Published by Karoline Dahrling Hughes 2023

Text, photography, and artwork copyright by
Karoline Dahrling Hughes

Thanks to Stinne Jensdotter for guidance and love.

www.skandimama.com
www.linasdatter.dk

To all the makers out there. Thank you for continuing to create beautiful things, inspiring each other, and sparking joy even though the world is burning.

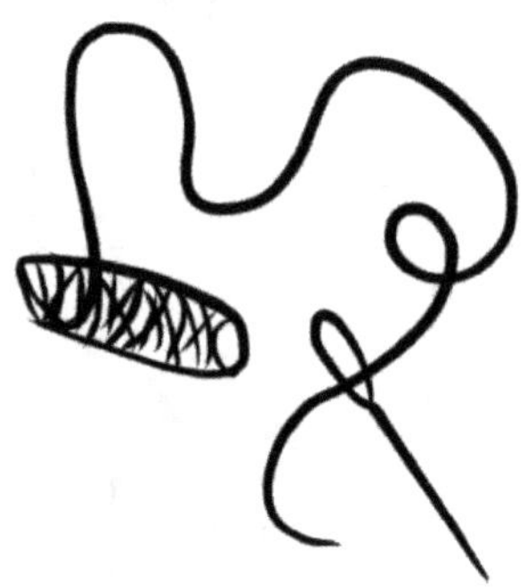

HOW TO WRITE AND PUBLISH A CRAFT BOOK

Welcome

Congrats on being here!

It is fantastic that you have chosen this book
and I am sure that you are on the way to
making a great craft book yourself.

Most likely, you love craft books and perhaps
you have a lot of them on your own shelves.
Or maybe you think that most craft books are
really not that well done and that you can

make a much better one. That is quite ok, and also a good reason to get started writing your own.

You are now embarking on the long and gruelling road to making a book and becoming an author. It is not a fast and straightforward way to get neither rich nor famous, so that should not be why you are doing it, but I am quite sure it is not. You probably have a great love for your craft and simply just want to share it with the world and inspire others.

It will be a long, hard journey but there are several rewards along the way - so I hope you will enjoy it.

Well done for being here. Let us begin.

You as an expert

The world of crafts is huge and there are so
many ways to do so many different things.
Since you are reading this book, I am sure you
must be some kind of expert.

Take a moment to take that in - The expert.
You.

Whether it is knitting, origami, weaving,
polymer clay, painting, or something else, I
am sure you are an expert in your field.
Perhaps not the only expert, and there will
surely be other experts out there who do
things their expert way, but you are some kind
of expert.
So, remember that along the way and silence
the negative voice inside of you. If you are not
hearing the negative voice now, I am sure it
will pop up and come along later. It most
often always does.

You have a right and a reason to want to write this book and show the world how to do the craft your way.

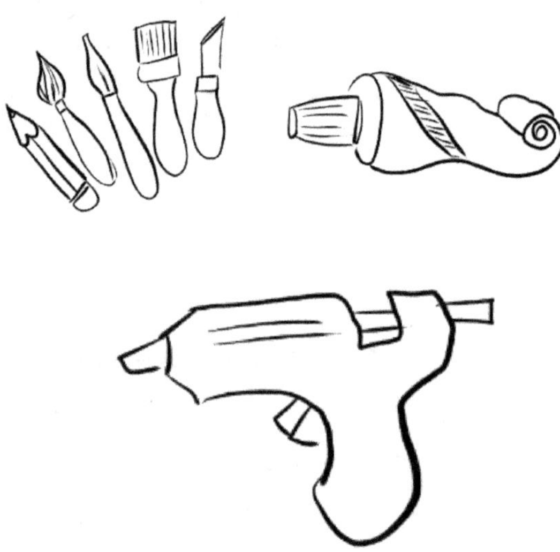

I have published many craft and sewing books, and I am in no way an expert of all things crafting and sewing. Not at all. I am quite bad at some techniques, and I am ok with that. But I am an expert in crafting and sewing my way. For example, I am an expert

on making fuss-free, no-pattern techniques
that help beginners who have no clue what
they are doing get started making clothes.

Readers and writers in other fields of for
example sewing may read my books and
think that I have completely missed the point,
but I know that I am good at doing my style of
sewing, and that is what I want to share with
the world.

Feeling OK about not being an expert in
every aspect is also vital in acknowledging
yourself as an expert in your specific field.

So, acknowledge it and celebrate it. And work hard at getting even clearer on what is your exact field of expertise.

Think about the following questions in regard to your field:

- How large is your field of expertise?
- Where are the limits?
- What exactly is it you know?
- Who can you help?

- What more could you learn to be even more of an expert?
- Is there something that makes you doubt yourself in particular, and how can you work around that or even immerse yourself in it?

Think about it again and this time write your answers down.

How large is your field of expertise?

....

....

....

Where are the limits?

....

....

....

What exactly is it you know?

....

....

....

Who can benefit from it?

....

....

....

What more could you learn to be even more
of an expert?

....

....

....

Is there something that makes you doubt
yourself in particular, and how can you work
around that or even immerse yourself in it?

....

....

....

This is what you will be working from.

And remember to celebrate the impressive wins along the way. Big and small. Document them for yourself, so you have proof that you are doing great for the moments you are feeling down.

You as a brand

-    And especially you as on online brand!

You might think now – *wait – I want to write and publish a craft book, why do I have to bother with thinking of myself as an online brand, right now?*
Because whether you like it or not, it is a crucial factor to calculate in for publishing houses looking at how easy it will be to sell your books. The number of active followers you have and how good you are at communicating will be a key factor when they assess as an author.
That is why having an online presence is particularly important. If you are already an important craft presence on the old interweb, your book will be a much easier sell.

And if you are new to being a brand online, you had better get started. Trying to get a book out there and find someone to publish it, people will Google you, and what do you want them to find?

Old Facebook photos from 2009? Some weird comment you made on a site that you have long forgotten about. Or an impressive blog, YouTube channel or Instagram account with all your expert advice and great stuff? The choice is yours. But try to Google yourself right now and see what comes up. Is it something that would be interesting to a future publishing house to check out? If not, then it is time to get to work.

No matter how tired you are of social media - and believe me, I get it if you are - there is just no way around it. Very few books get sold and very few author contracts get signed without it.

When selling a book to a publishing house, one of the key things they look at is whether you have a substantial number of followers who will be interested in buying your book. A publishing house will also look at how you present yourself, if you capture your audience and how consistent you are in posting because those are all things you will have to do to sell the book and work with them later on.

Help yourself and make sure you have an online presence.

I am all up for setting boundaries for yourself so think about how far you are willing to go and how much work you are able to put into it. Because honest to say, it will take some work.

The landscape of social media changes all the time, so figure out what you want to do with the trends that are happening right now.
Follow the ones you can and jump on any wagon you feel comfortable with - but remember to keep it sustainable for you.
You will not be able to do it all, even with several assistants on hand – which you probably will not have. So take your time into consideration and do the things that are fun. If you hate doing it, then you most likely will not be able to keep it up.
Doing the things you like makes it possible for you to keep doing it, and that is what you need to do.

You are your brand and having your name out there matters. People will Google you, and you can help decide what they see.

You - as creator, a crafter, and soon a writer – are a brand!
And everything that is visually you will be connected to you. That is why a good visual presence online is key. Whichever channels you choose.

Take those photos and videos - and make sure they are bright and great!

High quality photos and videos of yourself as a brand sounds corny, but it is especially important. For companies to want to collaborate with you, they need to see some instant value in your photos, videos and in your general image online. That does not mean that it has to be polished, fake or something that you would not consider YOU, but it does have to look good and be consistent. For brands to supply you with materials and exposure you should think about what you bring to the table. That could be impressive DIYS, the most creative ideas from their products, or beautiful styled shots of the package you just received from them. Without something to give in return it is not easy to find collaborators.

Bad shots do not sell anything. Least of all a book.

Make sure to have a good camera - it can be a DSLR, but newer phones will have great cameras and then you always have it with you. You will need a camera holder and a ring light, and sometimes perhaps a friend to help you as well.

But if you want to avoid being the person who always has to ask somebody to take photos of you, because I know that can be awkward, and my husband is not a fan of doing it, then get some stuff that can help you.
With a camera stand, a timer, or a timer app, you can take as many photos as you want without feeling weird about sharing the

moment, or you can practice talking and sharing on videos without feeling too self-conscious that someone is looking at you. Practice this, both for still shots, talking selfies or other videos. It takes some time and effort to become just somewhat confident in front of the camera but every time you pose it gets better.

Most people think they sound or look weird when they see and hear themselves on video, so do not worry about it.
Send small videos to your friends, evaluate out angles and how you come across on the screen. Soon you will get used to it and it will just be another part of the process of getting yourself out there.

To show off your brand, your person, and to communicate with your followers, it is also key that you show a bit of yourself behind the scenes. So when you are photographing all the things you know you should show off, remember to also show off a little bit about who you are. And make sure it fits in with your brand.

Your style - your brand - visual identity

Some people curate what they put online so that everything matches perfectly, but that is not necessarily how you need to do it. Your style can be more mixed and quirkier, but then be consistent in showing that.

Find your style, figure out what you want to
show, and then stick to it.
This does not mean that you cannot change
or that you have to limit yourself. But it is a
reminder to focus on how you want to be
perceived, how much you want to show, and
if your brand fits with the content of the books
you want to write.

If you are a creator of crazy pompom crafts is
that reflected in your personal style and the
visuals you show online? And if you are a
minimalist woodcrafter, does your visual

identity match that, or do you have online
clutter and mess that disturbs that look?
It is not to say that you need to be one-sided,
but you need to think about your choices.
Even if it is supposed to look completely
casual, creating that exact look will never
actually be that casual.

Find photos of yourself and crafts that have
the visual identity that you are striving for –
and others that can inspire you without
copying them. Make a mood board either on
paper or digitally and use it to be consistent.

Find out what defines you and figure out how you can be even clearer. Look at the things you love, the people you admire, and what your values are. See how it can all fit into your style and make people recognize you when they see your work online and in real life.

Your channels

It feels like every day a new app comes on the market, and there is a new and fun way to reach more followers. But chose your channels wisely. Do not do them all if you have not got the time. In that case it is better to choose some of the things. And when you read this book there might be more channels that are missing here. That is the evolution of the digital world. And do the ones you enjoy, because just like your craft it should be done with pleasure.

With your platform and your channels where you have your online presence, you can evaluate what your audience think about your projects, and – do people there care enough about the subject to want to buy a book about it? So that is why they cannot just be avoided.

In the following pages I will look deeper into some of the different channels.

Website / blog

A website or a blog can be an important thing to have. It can work as a landing page for you and with the right SEO (search engine optimization) it can work wonders for you.
If you are a crafter with an online presence perhaps you already have a blog, and you will know that trying to maintain it can be hard. So many other channels have taken over your

time and attention and it can be difficult to take time to create the proper SEO-correct content to put onto it.

If you have a blog that has not been updated for ages, that does not look good. But perhaps if your blog has run its course, it can still work for you. Change it slightly so that the landing page becomes a static presentation page about you, like a proper website, and keep the blog in the menu. That way you can still post occasionally, but it will not be as visible when someone checks in that it has been 5 months since your last post.

If you do not have a blog or a website, you can try WordPress and test it out yourself. It is not that difficult to set up, and when you become an author, it will be useful to have a site to publish all your news.

If you choose to have a blog (and I think that is an excellent choice because it will demonstrate to publishing houses the style of the DIYs you make), your blog must answer questions to create traffic. Think of what you do when you go to Google. You ask it a question and everything that pops up are answers to that. So, whenever you make blog posts you need to think about what question out there you are answering.

It is all about search engine optimisation and making the search engines work for you by using the right keywords. It is a bit hard to get into, but it is worth your while to do so. There are lots of SEO tutorials on YouTube that can help you dive into the world of how to write the proper text, make it the right length, using enough photos, making sure your posts have both links to other pages on your blog, and links to other sites as well, making sure you use the correct H1, H2 and H3 headlines, and much more. Maintaining a blog is not just putting out some lines and photos about a project, it is much more than that. But you can use it to your advantage.

I have some posts that perform really well SEO-wise, and it is a huge boost to see them rank so high when I Google "bandana dress" both in blogposts and YouTube content.

if you spend some time creating some very search engine optimised posts for you blog for questions in your field, you will be doing your best to being seen in your area of expertise. The best rule is to write and post original content that you would like to read yourself. Then most likely someone else will too.

YouTube

Video content on YouTube can also be helpful in building an online community and in practicing your presentation skills. Most likely your publishing house will want you to do instructional videos, LIVEs or Q&A's on their channels.

Just as your images need to be properly lit
and of good quality, your filming also needs
attention. It is a learning curve and nobody
begins as a videographer expert, but do pay
attention to the lighting, the sound and the
editing. Short videos perform well, so help
your viewings by cutting or speeding up the
boring or slow parts. Remember to speak
clearly and use a microphone if possible. Also
be sure to have sharp images.
It takes some time to learn, and I still
experience mistakes with images that are out
of focus, but the more you practice the better
it gets.

Instagram

Instagram is a wonderful place for crafters. If you want to collaborate with companies and other crafters, it is also an important channel for collaborations, so it is hard to be without. It is easy to show off both beautiful images of products and process in the grid, and stories is excellent for showing a bit of the day-to-day stuff that happens behind the scenes. You can ask questions, make reels and polls or do LIVEs to involve your followers. I suggest you do what you think is fun on Instagram because the algorithm changes so often. The best way to make the algorithm work for you is by being consistent, and that is most easy if you like what you do.

For many old school bloggers, Instagram took over and so many blogs have been forgotten because of it, and it has changed the way we consume content. Then TikTok grabbed everyone's attention and that is just to show how the social media scene will always change into something else.

Facebook pages and Facebook groups

Many crafters that do not have a website or a blog have a Facebook page instead. It is a terrific way to show content, images, videos, and links.
Facebook can also be used for making groups where you can tap into your community.

Facebook is great for having a page for your author's self, your content creator persona or perhaps just your personal profile, but it can also be awesome for a group where you connect to a community and make your own focus group.
Be sure to offer advice, give out content and offer a safe space for people to communicate with each other.

People interested in your field of expertise will be searching on Facebook for groups that can help them, so create that group and get their attention. By answering questions and being a helpful source, you will get more background for your expertise. You will also have a group of people interested in your area - and the book you will be publishing about it. It requires that you take the time to be part of your community but it also provides you with a trusting group of followers and a direct channel to reach them.

You can also join other groups in your field. There will be members asking questions you can answer, and you can also post there with links to any content of yours that gives helpful advice or offers a solution. Just be careful to not always do it with a link to one of your pages or products. People see through that and sometimes it is nice to just help others without turning it into a sell.

Pinterest

If you have a blog, a website or a YouTube channel, Pinterest is where you can pin images or videos so that people can find your content.
Pinterest works like a search engine, so be sure to write the proper keywords when you pin your content to Pinterest.

Pinterest is also valuable for gathering your own inspiration, as well as pinning other creative works. You will end up with different boards and followers who like the things you pin, both your own and others' content. When you create pins, you can take the images from your blogpost or thumbnails, but it works well to make special long narrow versions of these visuals for Pinterest since they work well in the Pinterest format.

Newsletter

A newsletter is a valuable tool in case your Facebook or Instagram gets hacked or closed down, because it is yours - you own it, just like a blog or website. Some content creators have been in that unfortunate situation and suddenly lost all their content as well as their entire community. With a newsletter you have your followers signed up to an email and you can reach them if you need to.

It takes time to set up the newsletter, and you should be absolutely true to yourself with how you want to use it. And be critical about how you treat newsletters yourself. Do you read them or pop them straight to the bin? If you are going to make your followers read your newsletter, what can you do to make it more interesting? Should you post it less often, do

you need to give away freebies or how should
you approach it?

I suggest you look at the newsletters you
actually read and see what they are doing
right, because I am sure that if you are just a
little bit like me, a lot of them also go straight
to the trash.

Examine why you read the ones you do and
see if you can work some of that magic too.

TikTok

TikTok is a great place to show off your craft
but it requires that you spend time both
looking at trends on the platform and making
videos yourself. That said, it can be a terrific
way to get out there and reach a new
audience with short format videos that show
who you are as a crafter and the skills you can
offer. Spend time looking into the content
and seek inspiration on trends and ideas, but

be careful to not get sucked in so all your
creative time disappears.

Making a podcast

Recording your own podcast is also a way to
reach your audience. What can you bring to
the table of expertise, skills, interviews with
others or fun stories? If you listen to other
crafting podcasts, perhaps you know whether
it is the descriptions of techniques or the
good chats to listen to in between that you
enjoy. While there are a gazillion websites,
Instagram accounts and YouTube channels,

there are not as many podcasts (yet), so this could be a way for you to tap into a new way of communicating with people who share your passion for crafting.
It requires a microphone and a bit of editing software, but nothing that should stop you from trying if it is what you want to do.

What to choose?

There are lots of other channels I have not gone through here and new ones pop up all the time. No matter how much you want to be on all of them, be aware that it takes time and effort. So choose wisely to where you want to be and dedicate your energy to that channel. Even though you can do some cross posting or recycle content, it still takes time to alter and post it.

A publishing house will without a doubt require that you be on social media and have a newsletter. It is up to you which ones you choose, but be prepared to explain your choices and why you have decided against some of them.
Make sure your choices make sense. If they make sense to you, they will make sense to your publisher too.

No matter the channel, remember to answer questions and write people back, both to help the algorithm but also to show your followers that you are interested in giving and not just in receiving likes.

And no matter the channel, be sure to post consistently. It does not have to be the same time every week or every day but be careful about not leaving your channels unattended for too long. If you do take a break from one of your channels, you can leave a message

explaining that so visitors will not be confused
that there is not any recent content.
And remember: It is OK to take a break if it all
gets too much.

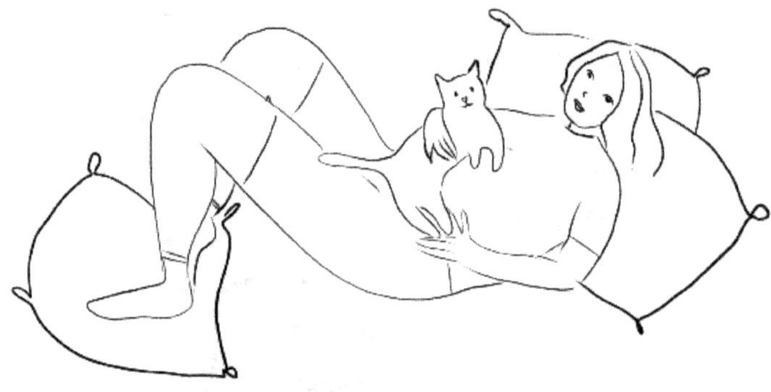

Other books in the field

Neither the paper nor the online book is dead, and more and more books come out with people being able to self-publish both digitally and in paper form. You are not the only one out there looking to publish a book – far from it.

But since we have established that you are an expert in your field, it's time to look at the other books that are out there. Perhaps your book needs to be published because it simply isn't there. Perhaps a version of it is out there, but just so badly written or outdated that you want to write the new version.

A gap in the market, something that is popular at the moment and still will be in a year or two, spiced up with your specific style could be exactly what is perfect for the book market. If your special niche can be mixed with an emerging trend or something that has recently become popular, then you could be onto a solid hit.

The most important thing for you is to really look around and see if you can find the same kind of content anywhere. A publishing house will be much more interested if you can establish that you are bringing something new – and needed - to the table.

But it is also important to look at the competing books. Who is the author, how old are they, how well have they sold, what is their style and target group. All those things are to be taken into consideration when you write your pitch of your book to the publishing house.
And it would be a shame to do a lot of demanding work if someone else has already written exactly what you want to write.
Perhaps you can still do it better but you will have a harder time convincing the publishing house that they need you.

If there are lots of books on the subject that can still prove to be an advantage though, since it will show that there is a market for books in that field. And if lots of books about the subject are already selling, perhaps you can convince a publisher to publish another one.

If you do that, it is especially important to be clear on what makes your book different.
Why is it that your book will be so much better?
What new angle will you see the subject from?
What new and coming trends will make your book sell in future years as well?
What can you bring to your book that another author can't?

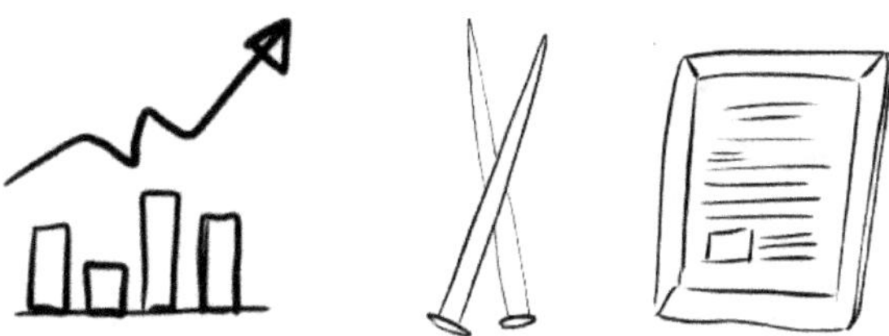

The key question is if there is a demand for your book and if you can document that demand. And this is where it comes in handy to have a platform with a community or followers, so you can prove that your subject is something that gathers interest.

Would they buy your book? That is an important question. And even more important, of course - would YOU buy your book? I am sure you would, because you are the expert, and that is awesome!

Target group

You are the expert in your field but who are your readers? Who is your target group?

It is a vital step to map out what your readers are like. The kind of books they read, the blogs they follow, the influencers they swear by. Not that you should copy anything, but it is useful to have a look at it and identify the matches with your area and brand.

Make a persona mapping of a person in your
target group. Draw them in a notebook,
digitally, make notes on your computer or
answer it right here:

Pick a name for them:

....

Profession?

....
....

Age?

....

Where do they live?

....

What are their hobbies?

....

....

What style do they like?

....

....

What do they dream of?

....

....

How do they value quality?

....

....

Do they have the time and energy to want
projects with lots of details or are they looking
for something simpler?

....

....

You can find images of people who could
look like your persona types that you can use
in the process, or you can make entire mood
boards on their style.

This does not mean that you cannot reach
someone outside of your persona group but it
gives you an idea about who you are
communicating with. If you have the time it
can also be helpful to make three different
personas so you can imagine how they would
all perceive what you are bringing out there.

Keeping your persona(s) in mind will make it
easier for you to make choices along the way

when you are authoring your book and choosing among different layouts and styles. It can even come in handy when you are deciding on a title – to wonder whether your persona types would pick up that book in a bookstore or a library.

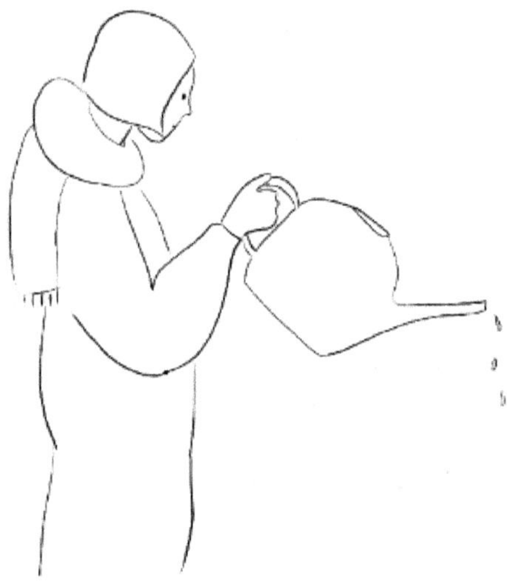

Making the book

As the expert you are you have probably
been gathering the information for this
book for quite some time.
Now it is time to put it all together.

The selling point – the best idea!

A good craft book needs to be sold on a great concept – the gap in the market or your brilliant new idea – but it still needs the right style and layout to work. So of course it has that brilliant thing, the other books are missing, but it also have the other important elements, we will look into now.

Photographs

For a craft book you need lots of visuals. The readers need to see how amazing the projects are with bright and beautiful photos. If you are going to take the photos yourself (which you can definitely do) you need to either up your photography game or align yourself with a great photographer if you do not want to stress about that point yourself. Make a contract on payment. You can pay a one-time fee or sign a contract that the photographer will get a certain share when the book comes out.

If you book models for the presentation shoots, make sure that they sign model permission forms, so you do not get in trouble afterwards. Your publishing house will most likely ask you to have them as a part of the package you hand over.

Instructions

The readers also need to be able to make the things themselves with the proper step by step instructions.

For this you can either do illustrations or photos along with a good written guide. Whether illustrations or photos are better depends on the type of craft.
If you have an iPad, you can use the Procreate drawing program to make illustrations but there are also illustration programmes like Adobe Illustrator that will allow you to make vector files of your illustrations with lots of possibilities for alterations.

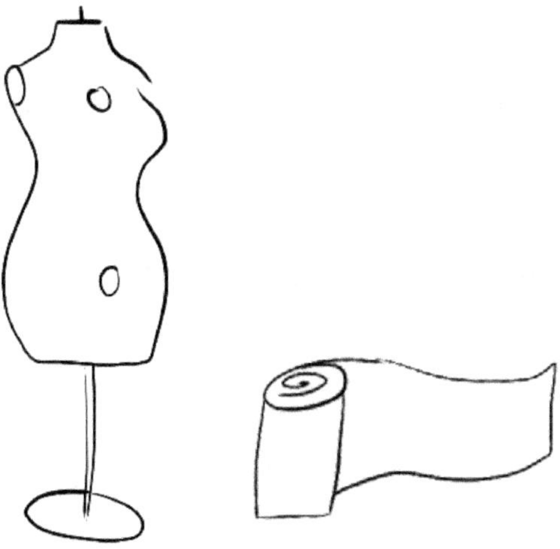

If you can do it yourself it might not be very difficult depending on the type of illustrations, but if you need to hire a freelance illustrator it will not be a cheap task.

Step-by-step photos can be very precise and useful and are easier to make yourself as you go along. If you need your own hands in the shot, you can use a timer camera and a stand.

It is a good thing to figure out beforehand approximately how detailed you want to make the step-by-step instructions. There is a significant difference layout-wise whether you will use four photos in one project and sixteen in the next. The more consistent you can make it, the easier the layout will be.

The content

Deciding on the content of the book is always exciting and my favourite part of the process. I scribble down ideas in lots of notebooks and draw out my ideas on big sheets of paper. I then use even more notebooks and post-it notes before the big final drawing.
Here I make a space for each project with space to write down what materials are needed and approximately what level the project is on. That way I will know later on if it should come in the beginning or later in the book.

For projects with fabric or yarn I like to pin small pieces of the material onto the big drawing.

In the drawing I can also make an estimation whether it is a 2 – 4- or 6-page project. That gives me an estimate on how long the book will be. If it is too short, I may need to add more projects.
I always use a one-page style shot and perhaps the step-by-step guide can fit on another page. If the instructions take up a lot of space, I will use 2 or 4 more pages. I prefer to begin new projects on a new double

spread, so I like to keep the page count for my projects even. But perhaps you make tiny easy crafts that can fit on just one page so you can fit two projects on a double spread.

If you are making something to be worn, it is also a clever idea to think about sizes for the projects. For my sewing book StyleHacking I had to be sure that I had made a large enough variety of sizes in the different projects. The big drawing helped me keep track of that.

At this point you can also make a mood board. This will help you keep track of colours and styles. Perhaps you want a soft pastel blue backdrop for your table or wall when photographing all the step-by-step photos, and if you use fabrics, beads, paint or paper, you may want a special colour scheme to go by.

I once tried to make a sewing book just by using leftovers from my stash, but the outcome was too messy. Eventually I had to clean it up. I could keep some of it, but I had to figure out a style to go with and buy new fabric that fitted into that to create a clear look. Luckily, some of the things I had made at first could be used in that look, but a lot of it also had to go.
That taught me to always start with a clear look on how the different projects will appear together. If they do not match at all, perhaps they need to branch out into several craft books instead.

Test- and proof reading

Think about the reader when you make the crafts yourself and think about how you will make the instructions as easy as possible for them to understand.
You are the expert so of course you know what you are doing but remember that you are showing it to someone who is potentially brand-new to the field.

If you can, have both someone who is new to the field as well as someone experienced check out your text along the way to see if it makes sense. This will help you see if you need to change direction before the entire book is done. And make sure to also get some help with grammar and spelling, so you are sure, there are no major errors.

Getting ready for the pitch

To sell the book you do not need to have it completely finished. Sometimes it is enough to just have a few of the ideas very clearly drawn out and the rest of it in the form of a synopsis, but the more you can have an overview of, the better. This also shows your publishing house that you have a plan.
Have a list of the content ready, even if not all the content is done. The publishing house also needs to have an idea about how many pages the book will be.

If you can to make a clean layout of the book yourself it makes it quite easy for the publishing house to see your ideas. It also helps you keep track of the process but do not spend too much time doing a whole graphic elaborate design. Most publishing houses have their own design teams and will probably want to layout the book so it fits with their different series of books, so dot spend time finishing it to perfection.

If you do want to be your own graphic designer to make everything look as good as possible before sending off the pitch you can use Adobe InDesign, Canva or other templates. You can also use a simple file in Word to show both the text and the images. Remember to save high resolution images of all the photos and illustrations.

Batch work

It is very necessary to be efficient and batch your work when you are making a book. The process includes so many tasks and unless you want it to take several years, batch working is simply necessary.

Most likely you will be making this book while you are juggling something else as well. Whether it is a job, an education, family life, loss or other tragic events it means that the book will not be the only thing for you to focus on. So when you have an afternoon, an evening or perhaps a whole weekend to work on your book project, it is important to be prepared and batch your tasks.

I usually prepare all my fabric in batches. First, I mark and cut the fabric. I also do the documentation in batch. When the lights and the camera are set up for that part it is easy to take all the pictures in one go. The rest of my tasks are also done in batch, all the way down to making a big sewing pile, and then sewing everything with white thread before changing to pink and changing to blue. Just to save as much time as possible and not have to change the thread back and forth constantly.

This means that you have to be well prepared and have your projects well planned out in advance.

It also means that not all the tasks are fun. There can be a whole afternoon of ironing, but then you know it will get done, and you can move on to a more fun task on the list afterwards.

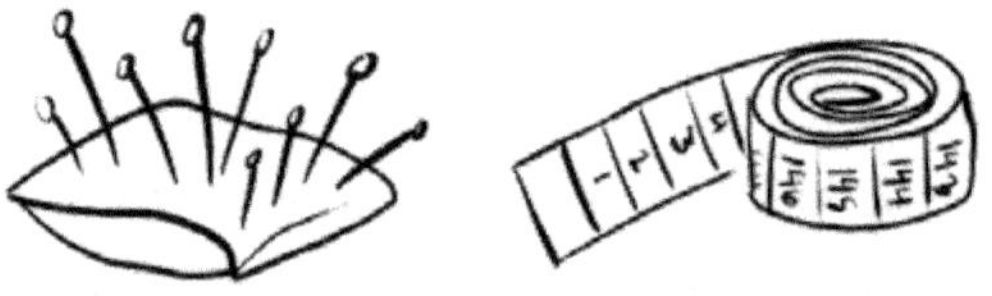

Sometimes, of course, it is not possible to do everything in batches, There will always be things forgotten or new ideas that pop up, but generally it is good to keep batch working in mind.

Types of batch working in this process could be:

- Mind mapping ideas
- Researching inspiration
- Researching styles and layouts
- Gathering materials
- Making templates, patterns, or other design types
- Writing step-by-step instructions
- Splitting up the creative process in various parts and doing them in batches
- Editing photos
- Editing text
- Preparing social media posts about the content
- Writing blogposts about the content
- Filming DIY videos
- Editing videos
- Shooting style and presentation shots for the book

- Writing letters to publishing houses (yes, in plural – you will most likely have to write to more than one publishing house)

Time plan

To make sure that it can all be done, it is vital to prioritise the tasks.

Make a time plan with everything you need to finish to make the pitch to make sure you get it sent off before someone else produces the idea and makes the book.

The first deadline is to finish the work for the pitch and send it off to publishing houses. While you are waiting for publishing houses to respond you can continue working on the content, but after you have signed the contract, you will have a new deadline. This will be for finishing the book.
Make a time plan for everything you need to do - both your own work but also the deadlines for the publishing house.
You do not want to miss those deadlines, because it might make your payment smaller if stated in your contract.

Prepare yourself for the process in the best feasible way because even though part of your book might write itself, some things in the process will be hard and require long nights at the desk.

Researching publishing houses

I am sure that since you are going to write a craft book you must also be a lover of craft books, and perhaps you already have some favourite publishing houses. Now is the time to thoroughly investigate that world.
I suggest that you go about it with some planning and make a list. Look through your own bookcase to start with, go to the library, but you can also browse online bookshops and look at book covers and content to see what looks right for you.

Last but not least, you can find lots of information on the Internet if you dig deeper.

You need to note the following about each publishing house:

- Name
- Website
- Contact info.
- Whether to send you pitch digitally or printed out in the mail.
- Which area of crafts they publish books about.
- What other books they have published that you already know.

- Links to other books they have published that you can check out.
- Names of books that you can mention in a pitch for being in the same field.
- Whether you can submit on your own or need an agent to submit.
- If there is anything in particular you need to add for the book pitch.

The more you can research to make your pitch more customised for the specific publishing house the better. Just like an employer does not like to receive a completely template-based application letter for a job, a letter to follow a book pitch also needs to be written with the publishing house in mind. That does not mean that you cannot use a template for parts of it, but it is important that you show some insight in what the publishing house has already published and actually check whether your style and your type of craft fit it with them.

Perhaps the publishing house publish books about your area of crafts, but in a completely different style and layout than you prefer. In that case you have to decide whether you still want to apply with them. Your initial thoughts on design might be changed a lot to fit into their range of books, and it is worth your while to consider in advance which changes you can accept and which you cannot.

I suggest making a page in a notebook or a Word file where you note down for each publishing house when you sent them a pitch, and when they replied. Also write down if they gave any reasons for turning you down. It is a good way to keep track of which publishing houses you have sent your pitch to and how they reacted. Many publishing houses are kind in their replies and it can be beneficial to write them back kindly and ask if they would be interested if you update your pitch, or if you can contact them in the future for other book pitches.

Getting a book published is not just a quick thing that happens overnight, so keep track of all mails and dates. Sending the same pitch to the same publishing house because you did not pay attention is a shame.

The book pitch – making a book proposal

For pitching children's book and most novels and other nonfiction you need a literary agent to pith for you. That means you cannot just send a book pitch to an email address yourself. Some of the bigger publishing houses also need agent for craft books, but many of the medium size to smaller publishing houses do not use agents for craft books at this time.
That is lucky for you, because you do not have to worry about attracting and getting an agent right away.

Pitching a book to a publishing house means that you do not have to send an entire

finished book to the publishing house but just
the most important things that they need to
know about the book – and you.
The book pitch is to quickly show them how
amazing your book will be and how relevant it
is.

What to include in a book proposal to make
the pitch:
- A working title
- Brief summary/concept of the book.
- Draft contents list
- Example of finished chapter with craft
  projects. Show examples to give the
  publishing house something to judge
  from. Remember they might not be

experts in your specific area. Add images, make it an easy layout to read.

- An overview of the book mapping out how many chapters and approx. how many pages.
- Your followers and you online brand (your, website traffic, social media stats other public appearances or books, connections with your followers.
- Your expertise – and why you should write this book, show proof, show your angle, style, and your connection to followers.
- Other books you have published.
- **Details on** what will make your book relevant in the future to secure longevity for your book.
- What books are similar to yours both by the publishing house you are writing to but also by other publishing houses – and how does your book

bring something new and better to the
readers

- What side products from your book
  could the publishing house benefit
  from? And yourself – courses, kits,
  online additions, online groups
- More book ideas from you that could
  be included in a possible series.

You can also include a mood board that show
the desired style of your book and your
followers – the future readers of the book. It
can perhaps be a Pinterest board that you
share a link to. This will come in handy later

when the book designer asks about your ideas for the style of the book. - even though it can happen, that it will all change when you start working with the publishing house.

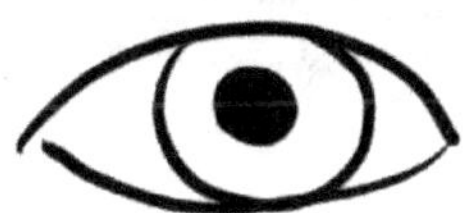

Many publishing houses prefer that you only send your book proposal to one of them at a time, but that can make the process awfully long. Most likely you will have to go through a certain number of no thank yous before you hit the jackpot, and many publishing houses take several weeks, sometimes months before replying. So I suggest that you can send the proposal to a couple at the same time, just to save yourself some time. If you are so lucky that two or more of all way to publish the book, it makes it possible for you to get the best deal possible.

Start sending it to the publishing houses that seems like the best fit, and that you most wish to work with and keep working down the list. Continue to research for publishing house along the way. New ones appear all the time.

Working with the publishing house

At some point you will receive that wonderful email with a positive reply that they like your idea and want to start collaborating with you. Even if you have sent them an entirely finished book it probably does not mean that they will just accept it as it is, and no matter what be prepared for a long process of collaborating. Perhaps they want to see more from you, read more chapters or want to see that you can change something in a certain direction, but if keep working in the same direction of making a book both you and the publishing house want to publish then you will probably sign that contract. And then you have a book deal! Congratulations!

As a first-time author you pretty much feel up for signing anything just to finally get a book out there.

It is important to look at the percentage that you get of the sales of the book, they can be anywhere from 7% - 15%, so as you can probably calculate you do not get rich quick on making craft books.

Some smaller publishers have better deals with up to 30% royalties to the authors but it is definitely not standard.

Some will also be willing to offer a certain amount in advance before the book is published, but for new authors the deals are not in their favor. You can try to make demands, but be careful what you want the

most, to fight over a certain percentage or to get your book published. Negotiating becomes much easier for the next books when you have more to negotiate with.
The publishing house also takes a chance on you, signing a new writer, and they know the market is uncertain.

Before you sign the contract make sure to read whether you give up the rights to your material for ever or for a certain number of years, that can be important for you, if you still want to sell patterns or tutorials in the future when the book is no longer in production.
Also note that some publishers automatically want to right to all of your images, so you

actually have to be careful where you use them afterwards.

Always get somebody to help you read the contract if possible. It is nice to have someone to go over it with. The publishing house will also be happy to make sure that you understand all the details, so they can also answer your questions.

It is not that the publishing houses want to trick you, because they naturally also want to have a good collaboration, but they just have standard contracts in the industry and you as the artist and crafter need to be very sure on what that means.

What you can use to negotiate an advance or a better percentage could be if you take all the photos and provide all the materials. Some crafters need the publishing house to set up photoshoots and illustrators to finish their books, and if you can provide a proper finish of the content they can save quite a bit of money on that . Money that should come to your advantage.

Working with a publishing house also means that you might have to kill your darlings and be open to constructive criticism. What you thought was the best part of your book, might be something they think should be changed. You will probably feel that they change your book in a direction that you do not want, but you have to trust that they also have a lot of knowledge about the market and what sells.

Saying that, it is still important to make your voice heard – even though you feel humbled by having required a book deal.
My first book in Danish was given an unbelievably bad title and I tried to go against it but did not push hard enough. I am still sure that a better title would have gotten it better sales, but the publishing house had not done a lot of books in that field and were not aware of the importance of SEO in the title as well. That made me vow to not give up so easily the next time.

For another book I wrote I did not think the initial design layout matched what I thought the readers would be attracted to, and even though the layouter might have been more than a bit annoyed with me, I still tried to push in the nicest possible way for some changes. It is a fine line between being a difficult "customer" in their shop, but if you have

knowledge about the market and the target
group it is vital that you speak up.

The publishing house will also have
knowledge about the same things, but it can
be a way to calibrate what you both know and
use your power together.

And remember -
If one publisher wants your book - perhaps
another one will too. And if you feel that the fit
is not right, then do not say yes.
Listen to your gut feeling and trust it.

And if all of this seems hard for you to do,
then having an agent could be what you

need. They can do the pitching and negotiate the contract, but they will also take a cut of your payment. You can search online for agents and apply to find the right one for you.

Don´t give up

Of course everybody should know when to quit, but do not let it be too early. Give yourself enough time to allow yourself to work on your project with all you have.

At some point in my life I realized I had had the same projects in the same drawers for several years, and that so much time had passed. Every new year I made a resolution that this year, I would work on that book or this book, but the year just went without me doing so. Why was that? Because it was overwhelming, I had so many projects to choose from, but also because times goes quickly for a busy person. At some point I decided that I needed to allocate my time to one of the projects and give it all I had for the next 6 months. That meant that I finally got somewhere. I made the choice to figure out which project to focus on, and then only worked at that. The more I got into it the easier it got, and I almost got a rush from accomplishing one task - one step on the way, which gave me energy for the next tasks.

I know you are probably busy and doing all
kinds of other important things in your life but
give yourself the gift of choosing one thing for
a while and decide how much time you want
to spend on it. Make a calendar and a strict -
but still realistic idea about how far you can
get in a certain amount of time.

Keep track along the way but be honest with
yourself when you get to the planned date.
If you have not completed it by then, then be
true to yourself about why. Why is it not done,
it is hard, do you procrastinate on this project

for some specific reason, and is it time to actually quit it?

I am not a fan of quitting, but at some point you also need to let some things go. Perhaps focus on another project, and you can come back to this, once your mojo is better, or you will have more experience to succeed with this project.

Do not give up on a book because nobody wants your book right now. Leave it off to the side for a while and work on something else and perhaps the publishing houses will be more open when you have other books out there.

Be consistent. Results are slow, and in this field there are no quick results.

So be kind and give yourself some time.
Remember that nothing is ever a waste of
time, it will always have brought some kind of
value to you.

Self-publishing

Perhaps there are no publishing houses
interested in your amazing idea. The market is
tough, and there will always be worries about
not selling enough books.
It is rough to get turned down at every door
but luckily there are still options for you and
your book.

The market of self-publishing has grown so much over the last couple of years.

And it can be a wonderful way to get your material out there, but since you do not have a publishing house backing you, you need to work hard on the marketing yourself.

Some publishing houses offer up deals to help you publish your book, but with a payment from you. It should not be the first thing you choose, but it can be an option if you publishers are not giving you any standard contract offers.

Some writers also offer up their book material as online courses. It can basically be the same type of content as in a book, but as a slideshow, a pdf or perhaps a presentation mixed with slides and video.

The best thing about it is, that you can sell it through your website and you get all the profit. But of course it is different from a real, printed book, if that is what you are looking for.

If you are looking to self-publish both as an eBook and a printed book, you can look to Amazon Kindle Direct Publishing or Ingram Spark. That is exactly what I went for with this book. I did not have the patience to look for a publishing house, because I wanted the book out straight way. So this book is entirely homemade and uploaded to Amazon Kindle Direct Publishing and Ingram Spark, so that it can either be downloaded for Kindle or printed on demand when paid for in your Amazon basket or ordered by book stores for you to buy.

With self-publishing you can write and layout the book yourself and the platform of your choice. You are then given a minimum prize and then you set the eBook and the printed version price after that. Since this book is without color images, it can be printed fairly cheap, but if you go for a book with color photos and illustrations it will up the price a lot.

For the eBook there are no costs, so the earnings from that can be particularly good.

There are lots of sizes to choose from, qualities of paper and types of cover material. Many use Amazon KDP to design low content notebooks, which means that you can now go onto amazon and find notebooks and planners on pretty much anything. But it is also brilliant if you have a book with proper content to publish.

Note that you have to layout it yourself or find someone who can help you, and that it is worth to do that properly to make it look as professional as possible.

You should also put effort into the cover - because we do judge books by their covers. Perhaps make a few suggestions and show them in your different channels. It is a fantastic way to get people to participate, but you could also get useful knowledge from it. Remember to also get a proof reader in to help you.

All the things that a publishing house would normally help you with is now totally on you. That also means selling the book - which means you have to be even more active on social media.

Having your own self published books and
eBooks, can also be a way to show the
publishers that you have a back catalogue
and something they can judge you from.
Perhaps a successful Amazon KDP book or
several sold courses will convince them, that
they should look further into your work.

Marketing and selling the book.

The publishing house will most likely want you to do a lot of publicity for them. That can be LIVES, Q&A, takeovers and more for the publishing house - both before to create hype and after the launch of the book. Take all those jobs with a smile and remember they can help get your book even further out here. If you feel things are a bit slow, ask the publishing house how well the book is doing and ask what you can do to help promote it more.

If you self-publish then remember that all this is up to you to plan and do, so be sure to keep up the clever work.

Creating a sell in advance by offering something for free

If you are self-publishing and have enough material to make a free downloadable pdf, online course, or eBook, and well as a craft book, you can use the first mentioned to create some attention around your subject. Making a free teaser with a couple of projects and an introduction can get people excited and you can use it to build your following. With many downloads you can show to a publishing house, that there is a demand for your work. Of course you have to be sure, that you have enough individual projects to still make an interesting book, and that you do not give all the best ones away for free.

A free download - " a freebie" can also be used to invite people to sign up for your newsletter or as a follower.
But remember that it is now enough to keep people there. If you spam them with too much content after, you can lose them just as quickly as they signed up.

Keep creating and writing

Writing and publishing a book is a huge win and proof to that inner critic of yours that you are a proper writer and remember that when you are in doubt.
But no matter what you do, there will always be negativity and sometimes trolls out there. There will be bad reviews, and no matter how tough it is learn as much as you can from them.

Keep in mind that you cannot please everyone, some people will have had a difficult day, some will have misunderstood, some will be envious, and some will not have given it enough time. Some might not like

your look or the style of the book. It is ok to
not be perfect for everyone.

I wish you so much luck with your book and
your future as a writer.

Karoline was born in 1981 in the Northern part of Denmark. Since a young age she has been crafting, painting and making with everything she could get her hands on.

Karoline has published *StyleHacking, Sew a Creative Wardrobe: Use 5 Favorite Garments for Limitless Possibilities* with C&T Publishing in 2021.

Since 2017 she has published more than 10 sewing and craft books as well as childrens books in Danish.

Visit Karoline Dahrling Hughes here:

www.skandimama.com

www.linasdatter.dk

www.instagram.com/karoline.skandimama

YouTube: Karoline Skandimama DIY